Illumen
Winter 2024

Edited by
Tyree Campbell

Illumen
Winter 2024

Edited by Tyree Campbell

Cover art "Cyberpunk Blue" by Sandy DeLuca
Cover design by Laura Givens

Vol. XXI, No. 2   January 2023
Illumen [ISSN: 1558-9714] is published quarterly on the 1st days of January, April, July, and October in the United States of America by Hiraeth Publishing, P.O. Box 1248, Tularosa, NM 88352. Copyright 2024 by Hiraeth Publishing. All rights revert to authors and artists upon publication except as noted in selected individual contracts. Nothing may be reproduced in whole or in part without written permission from the authors and artists. Any similarity between places and persons mentioned in the fiction or semi-fiction and real places or persons living or dead is coincidental. Writers and artists guidelines are available online at www.albanlake.com/guidelines. Guidelines are also available upon request from Hiraeth Publishing, P.O. Box 1248, Tularosa, NM 88352, if request is accompanied by a SASE #10 envelope with a 60-cent US stamp. Editor: Tyree Campbell. Subscriptions: $28 for one year [4 issues], $54 for two years [8 issues]. Single copies $10.00 postage paid in the United States. Subscriptions to Canada: $32 for one year, $54 for two years. Single copies $12.00 postage paid to Canada. U.S. and Canadian subscribers remit in U.S. funds. All other countries inquire about rates.

New from Terrie Leigh Relf!!
Postcards From Space

Terrie Leigh Relf loves sending and receiving postcards from the four corners of the universe—and beyond! Postcards tell a story. They are mementos from friends and family—and from total strangers—and provide a glimpse into life's journeys, observations, and adventures.

Here are some messages on postcards from space, found aboard a derelict craft that crashed on an arid, lifeless world. The OSPS (Outer Space Postal Service) has delivered these messages to Terrie, who now presents them to you. This is what it is like out there.

https://www.hiraethsffh.com/product-page/postcards-from-space-by-terrie-leigh-relf

A Little Help, Please

In the world of the small indie press we fight a never-ending battle for attention to our work, as writers and in publishing. Here's an example: big publishers [you know who they are] have gobs of $$$ that they can devote to advertising and marketing. Here at Hiraeth Publishing, our advertising budget consists of the deposits for whatever soda bottles and aluminum cans we can find alongside the highways. Anti-littering laws make our task even more difficult . . . ☺

That's where YOU come in. YOU are our best promoter. YOU are the one who can tell others about us. Just send 'em to our website, tell them about our store. That's all. Just that.

Of course, we don't mind if you talk us up. We're pretty good, you know. We have some award-winning and award-nominated writers and artists, plus other voices well-deserving to be heard [not everyone wins awards, right?] but our publications are read-worthy nevertheless.

That number once again is:

www.hiraethsffh.com

Friend us on Facebook at Hiraeth Publish and follow us on Twitter at

@HiraethPublish1

Contents

Features

17 The Guy Belleranti Page
22 Book Review: The Uber Cat and Dragon Owner Manual Reviewed by Lisa Timpf
26 Featured Poet: Alexis Child
41 The Simon Kewin Page
47 Who's Who

Poems

10 Cuppa Bardo by n a spencer
11 Stygian Night by Anthony Bernstein
12 The Mother of Lands by Iuliia Vereta
13 Phantom Heart by John Philip Johnson
16 Detached by Debby Feo
18 The Demon of the Islands by Frank Coffman
19 new world by Greg Schwartz
34 Threshold by n a spencer
35 Serpentine Reflections by A. D. Walke
39 Forgotten and SL4 by Debby Feo
40 In Line for Weekly Rations by John Philip Johnson
42 Reappearing by Iuliia Vereta
44 Messenger by n a spencer
45 Our Compound by John Philip Johnson

Illustrations

16 Detached by t.santitoro
38 Forgotten by t.santitoro

SUBSCRIBE TO ILLUMEN!!

We'll be glad you did...
So will you.
Here's the link:

https://www.hiraethsffh.com/product-page/illumen-1

Support the small independent press!

You're not afraid of a little poetry, are you?

The Miseducation of the Androids
By William Landis

What happens when androids confront concepts inconsistent with their programming? William Landis examines this question by means of flash fiction and haiku that you will find pithy, poignant, and amusing.

William Landis is a science fiction poet from North Carolina. He is a graduate of North Carolina A&T State University, completing both undergraduate, and graduate work in agriculture. He is currently working on a vermicomposting project, and he is an Army reserve engineer officer. He enjoys running, writing, reading, and exploring new places.

Order a copy here: https://www.hiraethsffh.com/product-page/miseducation-of-the-androids-by-william-landis

Midnight Comes Early
By Marcie Lynn Tentchoff

Marcie Lynn Tentchoff lives on the west coast of Canada, in a forest of brambles and evergreens far too densely tangled to form the setting for any but the darkest of fairy tales. She writes poetry and stories that tiptoe worriedly along the border of speculation and horror, and is an active member of both the Science Fiction & Fantasy Poetry Association and the Horror Writers Association. Marcie is an Aurora Award winner, and her work has been either nominated, short, or long-listed for Stoker, Rhysling, and British Fantasy awards. She is very much involved in middle grade and YA media, and edits Spaceports & Spidersilk, a magazine aimed at readers from 8-9 up to (and past!) 89. When she is not involved with the practice of placing and editing words on a page, she teaches creative writing and acting for a performing arts studio.

Order a copy here...

https://www.hiraethsffh.com/product-page/midnight-comes-early-by-marcie-lynn-tentchoff

Cuppa Bardo
~ n a spencer

The mind was dreaming. The world was its dream ...
~ Jorge Luis Borges

The shrinking dog days of September
Leave me just a little breathless
                        waking up
To a layered haze of milky ruminations
Clouding the coffee inside my cup
                        as tho'
I were little more than like a cloud myself
Spread across an indelible horizon

Embracing the whole chingaso
                        cup and all
Just that way the eye doubles back inside itself
To ring the world disclosed before its gaze
With its own ineluctable reflection

                        as palpable
As the touch of warm ceramic on my fingers
As I lift the cup to my lips
                        coffee and cream

Sip by sip
          a barrelful of monkey milk
That in reality is drinking me

Stygian Night
Anthony Bernstein

No shadows are cast
    on this stygian night
No silvery orb
    reflecting luminous favor
No shimmering horn
    by which the angels may steer
Nor fair concubine
    to stave off this mad winter
No chance for redemption
    but burning desires
No wings for the phoenix
    nor starscape to soar to
No muse to inspire
    no verse to delight
Nor song to lull sweet
    through this stygian night

The Mother of Lands
Iuliia Vereta

Devastated, desperate, we sat there
on the sands of artificial moons, scorched
by the almighty sun and wept, remembering
the Earth, its winds, verdure and dew.

There those who captivated us demanded
from us words of the songs, we sang when
we were kids, captains from old books, -
songs we sang rushing faster than light;
oppressors never heard the ringing, with which
we laughed undertaking campaigns and fights.

But how can we sing the song of the Earth
on the strange sands? If I forget you, Mother of Lands,
I'll cut off my right hand and stick my tongue
to my throat. If the day comes when I do not
    remember,
if I do not want to bring back everything we had,
light pillars and merry dancers, shining like
    stroboscopes,
then let the tripods suck out my bone marrow
and stem cells, leaving me to die on the stone, hard
like the new land we were trying to settle on and
    failed.

Phantom Heart
John Philip Johnson

It's like not having a body,
this floating you find yourself in
without a universe around you.
It is nothing. No sight,
no sound, no air pulling in and out
of your lungs, nothing but
the amorphous drift of your thoughts
and the quaint sensations—
more like imagining—
of the movements of your many
phantom limbs.
They flail in the mind's eye
of how you remember them,
but already your memory is failing.
Bits of yourself are seeping
into what you cannot know.
Place has left your body.
Now your mind is leaving too.
You are disappearing.

Planet Hunter
By Alan Ira Gordon

Alan Ira Gordon is an urban planner and urban studies professor at Worcester State University and writer of science fiction/fantasy short stories and poetry. He's a three-time Rhysling Award nominee and a Dwarf Star Award nominee. He's contributed to several publications of Hiraeth Publishing, is a frequent contributor to Star*Line and guest-edited Issue #24 of Eye To The Telescope, the on-line publication of the Science Fiction & Fantasy Poetry Association (SFWA). His poetry, short stories and articles have been published in various genre magazines and anthologies, a partial list of which can be found on his webpage at www.alaniragordon.com.

Get a copy here...

https://www.hiraethsffh.com/product-page/planet-hunters-by-alan-ira-gordon

Detached
Debby Feo

Her injured wings felt detached
As if not a part of her
Desperate dragon stranded
On a distant asteroid

The Guy Belleranti Page

spilled trick or treat bags
witch's broom sweeps up sweets
gives children rides

civilized monster
remarkably romantic
eats prey by candlelight

art exhibition
canvases running red
critics running, too

mad neurosurgeon
cracks open another skull
wants to read minds

The Ripening

I climb higher and higher,
taking my time to study
each budding branch.

Other family members will soon join me,
for numerous buds are ripe,
and many fingers will be needed
to pick the next generation
from our family tree.

The Demon of the Islands
(the explanation of a famous mystery)
Frank Coffman

"This human lot is alien to this land.
Their island is not this—my own domain.
The natives on these islets understand
That—only by my will—may they remain.
These foreigners are too haughty to come here!
It makes my scales crawl and my blood run black!
So, I must reveal myself—feed on their fear
When they perceive there is no going back.
Forsooth, the Demon of these Lands am I.
Their camp, their ilk I will obliterate!"
                    * * *
"Now only ghosts and their crumbling dwellings lie
Here where these foolish settlers met their fate."
                    * * *
*These were the words dread Croatoan spoke
Before and after 'cleansing' Roanoke.*

new world
Greg Schwartz

drifting
through space
cryogenic sleep
disjointed dreams
strung together like cobwebs
multiple realities
all at once
and never
and shouldn't ever be

then you wake
arrive
on a new world
new life
those crazy dreams
fade to gray
dwarfed
by a new reality
a giant surreal painting
that you've somehow melted into
nonsensical and alien
but also
home

In Days to Come

By Lisa Timpf

The poems in this collection are grouped into four sections. The first, "Terra, Terra," includes poems set on the planet Earth. That is true of many of the poems in the second section, "Looming Shadows," though they have been grouped together in relation to some of the potential disasters we as a human race have set ourselves up for—nuclear warfare, climate change, and so on. "Alien Encounters" contains poems relating to imagined interactions with other space-faring species. "Other Worlds" rounds out the collection with speculations on what life might be like if and when humanity spins out to the stars.

Order a copy here...
https://www.hiraethsffh.com/product-page/in-days-to-come-by-lisa-timpf

The Uber Cat and Dragon Owner Manual
by Marge Simon and Mary Turzillo
Reviewed by Lisa Timpf

Readers who have been seeking the ultimate manual on the care and feeding of pet dragons and magical cats need look no further. In *The Uber Cat and Dragon Handbook: A Pet Owner's Guide,* authors Marge Simon and Mary Turzillo offer all the necessary advice in a succinct and humorous manner.

The book is organized into sections, such as "Choosing Your New Pet," "Exercise," "Grooming," and other helpful topics. The pieces themselves come in a variety of forms, including poems, illustrations, flash fiction, and humorous articles purporting to be non-fiction. There are even lists, like Turzillo's "More Ways to Tell If Your Cat Is a Space Alien, " which includes indicators such as, "You find long distance charges on your telephone bill to area codes the operator has never heard of," and, "You come home to find your cat walking on the ceiling, and your cat just looks at you and says, 'Yeah, so?'"

Some of the poems are satirical takes on familiar songs. One such, Simon's "Streets of Toledo (The Dragon's Song)" includes the lines:

> Oh, pray you must tell me now where is your owner
> and pray tell me true did you lose all his dough?

Turzillo's "Invisible Cat," a poem about a phantom feline, contains a haunting note: "Phantom feline lives with you / He eats your food, he haunts your flat." "The Hunter's Mothers," also by Turzillo, portrays life from a cat's perspective:

She cut meat that she had caught
somewhere, and put it on plates as big as me
for her other kitttens, the large bald ones.
But she never let me have the knife,
nor let me play with the meat. Was I unworthy?

In "Your Darling New Dragon" Turzillo sagely reminds owners, "Remember, that cute dragon chick dragging your station wagon around as a pull-toy will very quickly become a playful forty-foot adolescent." In the "Training Dragons" section, Simon advocates the following method for teaching a dragon to lie down as a precursor for flight training: "Using a dragon dummy, gently lower it to a prone position. Then pretend to get on it. This has worked in 1 out of 10,000 cases, but stick with it. Sooner or later, the dragon will get the connection."

Though *The Uber Cat and Dragon Handbook* was first published more than ten years ago, I only ran across it recently. The book is fairly short—just under 70 pages—but it packs a lot in a small space. As a former cat owner, I found the cat pieces to be dead-on, and the dragon lore fits with how I might imagine dragon behaviour. Witty and satirical, *The Uber Cat and Dragon Handbook* provides fun fodder for feline fans and dragon devotees.

The Uber Cat and Dragon Owner Manual
By Marge Simon & Mary Turzillo

Do the curtains burst into flames when your dragon sneezes? Is the dragon litter box cluttered with fragments of princess tiaras? Has the cat sabotaged the TV remote so that you can only watch cat food ads? Do feline vixens use the scratching post for late-night pole dancing? Do you find yourself wandering aimlessly about the house, crying out, "Who's in charge of this place, anyway?"

    Cats and dragons do not come with owner's manuals. You have to buy these separately--and trust me, cats and dragons have planned it that way from the get-go. If they can keep you from buying this book, the answer to the question you keep crying out is, "Them!"

So buy this manual. Study it carefully. You still have a chance to get some semblance of your life back.

Endorsements:

On Oriental Ubers -You'll adore your baby Persian Faust. Kittens retain their fluffy cuteness for centuries before turning against their owners. At that time, it's advisable to leave.

"In this groundbreaking study, Professors Simon and Turzillo expose the needs of these amazing creatures. Both have been nominated for the Nobile Prize. Unfortunately, Turzillo hasn't been seen since filming her Dental Care for Smilodons documentary, while Simon has fled the US to live in a heavily armed compound in Athabasca."
--Dr. Floofy Le Strange, Dean, Cronell Veterinary School

"I really loved it, especially the part where the cat tried to eviscerate the dragon." -- Buffy V.

"If these two charlatans think they can loose the hordes of hell on America's families and call them pets, they've got another think coming. We have bazookas and will shoot to kill any giant cats or mutant reptiles on our streets."
--Poppy Z Fright, People Against Terrifying Animals

https://www.hiraethsffh.com/product-page/uber-cat-dragon-owner-manual-by-marge-simon-mary-turzillo

Featured Poet: Alexis Child
Wolf's Bane

Endymion I call your name

A dark sun is above us

We will dance upon days

Time has forgotten

Gazing at angels

Writing lullabies in the stars

You open your eyes

To the secrets that imprison you

In the wakeful anguish of the soul

The wolf's bane blooms

You are sweet and intoxicating

With wolf's bane blood

And hemlock eyes

Do you hear my world-weary cry?

You are asleep in a devil's dream

Cursed by the moon

Like the unforgiving world

I know you are waiting

You beckon in the dead of night

You've drowned your sorrows

Above the dreaming hills

The wind whispers, '"follow me"'

In secret tongues

With swords as lips

You await your lunar lover's kiss

I will not leave you at the end

Of the world

For death knows no one

I am certain of what you

Are praying for

I will awaken you from slumber

To sing your immortal song

Now let me in the door

War Dance

You are the key that unlocks shadows

The magick in these bones

Perhaps you are even the collector of souls

You reign over demons

And in your fury

Even death shudders in fright

Autumn bends to your furious will

A Messiah rises like a blood moon

Throughout the gloom

Echoing the war cry

You devour the world

You swallow the stars

You make them bleed

Ankh-f-n-khonsu

Hope in us cowers

With a penchant for madness

The flesh of mankind covers

The bone

War tears through the night sky

Horus, feathers of fire

Angel in disguise

Dance in my darkness

Waltz through the night

Strike me with your sword

Of light

To say so little hurts

For I am the wound

And you are the slap

The horror creeps

The devil is ice

I am devoured by the dragon

Look, my children
To the blood moon
Alive with wild magick

And you'll know it's your
Bedtime soon
Be gentle with me as I bleed

Deadly Nightshade

I have a deadly nightshade
It was akin to our first kiss
Your eyes are as dark
As Belladonna's berries
The torch we carry
Is a madman lunatic
Shackled in prisoner chains

We wither away

In a garden that never grows

It seems that you're deadly

Eat of the plant and leaves

The poison will appease me

I am angry with my foe

In a garden that never grows

Where the heart is tiny and broken

Stabbed by demons

I need your light

In a garden that never grows

That strangles the night

You are my own Atropos

Like the prisoners of whom I write

The Mystic Rose

The Alchemist burned her life

so she might seek fire and find passion

Within her soul, distraught.

Flawed by blood and bone deep within,

Fiery embers glowed.

I am enough fire all on my own (just like you).

O let our light and darkness mix,

my beauteous one. Rise up

From the ashes of failure.

Burn the old memories to the ground.

It only takes a spark to ignite the flame.

Remind me again why we

Feel lost with the stars up above?

Come closer, come closer though

I appear as ice.

Enthralled by orange light and reckless smoke,

The Holy Ghost with white wings,

grandeur of God changes

The lifeless wine of grief to living gold.

The petals of divided light,

although in pain shall be like your eyes,

The stars, a perfectly overflowing cup

raising Spirits up, our Venus.

Beyond the echoing ashes of the past,

with ashes of loss, we arise

And find mercy in the afterglow.

If tomorrow starts without me,

And I am not here to see it, do not weep.

I shall belong to the world

Of no end, the mother of fate in the dawn

where the Universe sleeps

Without delusion or dream.

In the voyage of vision, I am lifted up

From the abyss of my heart

to the Lord and Lady, swimming away

From the cauldron of my woes.

Alexis Child hails from Toronto, Canada; home to dreams and nightmares. Alexis is a former Social Service Worker, befriending the demons that roam freely amongst her writings. Her fiction and poetry has been featured in numerous online and print publications. Besides having rare mystical experiences she hopes are not just short circuits in the brain, she offers Tarot Readings and writes fiction and poetry, starving in the garret with her muse. A starving child is a frightful sight. A starving vampire is even worse. Please donate non-perishable food items and B-negative blood (and make it a double!).

Alexis' first collection of poetry, Devil in the Clock, a dark and sinister slice of the macabre is available on Amazon. Her second collection of poetry, Singing the Bones, is also available on Amazon. Her third collection of poetry, Exquisite Corpse is coming soon from Cyberwit Publishing. You have been warned...

Please Visit Alexis' YouTube Channel:
https://www.youtube.com/channel/UCg6S5u4yX73kA1ZWGnKaEBA/videos

Minimalism:
A Handbook of Minimalist Genre Poetic Forms

This handbook contains articles about how to write various minimalist poetry forms such as scifaiku, senryu, sijo, haibun, empat perkataan, ghazals, cinquain, cherita, rengays, rengu, octains, tanka, threesomes, and many more. Each article is written by an expert in that particular poetry form.

Teri Santitoro, aka sakyu, who assembled this handbook, has been the editor of Scifaikuest since 2003.

https://www.hiraethsffh.com/product-page/minimalism-a-handbook-of-minimalist-genre-poetic-forms

Threshold
~ n a spencer

The senses give rise to the body
The sense of it
          literally
Lending shape to the mind

As an eddy in the current
                        and an echo
Stitching back behind the wash
A thread of memory and anticipation

Where neither past nor future
Are anywhere to be found
                        but only *this!*
Like reaching out to grab at rainbows

Forever at a threshold
                        ever ghosting itself
                        and you
Ever playing catch-up in a rearview mirror
Flying or falling
                    with nowhere to stand

Swallowed up in the slipstream of a needle
As inexorable as a dream

Serpentine Reflections
A.D. Walke

I am queen of dusty earth,
poisonous heat, and
a profound nothingness.
My temple burns
on the edge of hell,
the Phlegethon pours forth
fumes and smoke
to obscure a forgotten sky.
It is a liminal space sought
only by heroes and fools -
the boundary of Hades' realm
he, a more just ruler than his
violent and philandering brothers.

Stone men offer me tribute
with their crumbling fists,
broken cocks, and
dead hearts.
With eyes I consume sacrifice.
First, hubris - strutting,
confident in his control.
Then, their ignoble intent,
pierced through with
unseen arrows.
Finally, sharp, sour fear -
when, stiff and impotent,
they finally behold what
they have created.
All pay the debt of the great thief
who sunk my stars in the wine dark sea.

It was another time,

another temple,
another goddess.
Sisters in cotton shifts
laughing in the white sun.
Work-browned arms swimming
through sticky, salted air,
dancing in the lacy foam
embroidering the waters.
I had stayed behind
to tend the fires.

A crack of thunder called me
outside to a darkening sky,
a threat in the chill wind.
Tide took on substance,
grasped greedily at my ankles,
dragged my legs from beneath me, then
crushed my body against the marble steps.
Cold brine washed
my Lady's name from my lips,
filled my nose,
burned my eyes,
pushed insistently between my legs.
Blind, violated, drowning...

Gray gulls cried in the cloudy sky.
I could not.
Tears belonged to the sea,
and I had my fill of salt.
I pulled my battered body
into the shadowy temple.
Heavy, bloodied legs
trailed behind me like
a land-murdered mermaid.
Panic mingled with pain -
must rekindle the fires,
relight the snuffed torches...

Then the flames flared to life
of their own accord.

My Lady tended my wounds
as one of my sisters -
ablutions,
anointing,
absolution.
How tenderly she sealed
my reddened thighs
with golden scales.
Combed my damp hair
with her battle-scarred fingers
leaving behind the
susurrations of serpents,
our minds now one.
She kissed my torn lips,
my bruised eyelids,
and blessed my vengeance
with immortality.

Tellers of tales call me cursed
as if beauty could ever be a virtue.
But punishment will always
be a matter of perspective,
and in my domain
of solitude and stone
even gods fear to tread.

Forgotten by t.santitoro

Forgotten
Debby Feo

I'm dead
Floating

What happens next
Waiting

Still floating

Words forgotten
Still unknown

People have moved on
I haven't

Floating

SL4

Tiny purple stones
Sentients in plain sight
Below sycamores

~Debby Feo

In Line for Weekly Rations
John Philip Johnson

I pretend his name is "Hank"
but I've never actually asked. It's better
if you don't know. But he's always
the one shoveling out wilted produce,
the leftovers so many of us live on.
He has become for me the face
of this gray, concrete warehouse.

Do you have any strawberries?
I ask quietly.
I don't ask it every time.
You have to be careful.
But once in a while he does.
That's the extent of our conversation,
two human
beings briefly united.

Today he pauses and nods.
Yeah, just for you.
It's almost a joke; I almost laugh.
He leans under the table
and pulls out a package.

Rubies. Gleaming red.
His eyes light up as he passes them,
and I can feel life in my own.

I accept them like a smuggler,
and even risk a nod before I shuffle
toward the stale bread station. I wonder
what name Hank
has for me.

The Simon Kewin Page

piano notes play
echoing in empty rooms
no piano there

through the telescope
shadow blotting out the stars
larger and larger

words in dripping red
white walls of a room kept locked
you won't leave alive

the creak of floorboards
footsteps in the room upstairs
yet you are alone

Reappearing
Iuliia Vereta

Let's go to Gliese, Katherine, -
shuttle from Boston, and there
we will reach downtown on dogs.
Here, waiting for a salary, you forgot
That you promised to buy my best suit.
We will be able to manage being casual.

Let's go to where the seagulls
fly under the raincoats and sit still
warming themselves in the squares.
And maybe I will remember the times
When our threadbare hearts were not yet
Disassembled into seventy-eight equal parts.

Summer is crying in color there.
We'll go back to the old half-made
world, where we could still afford our
hearts to be open, before being clad in ore.
We will roll everything back and remount life
correctly, without pauses and unneeded takes.

We'll cut their sky with a utility knife,
and it will spill, cracking by the power of
forty thousand rains, Katherine, and with
the best of Talking Heads and a noose around
the neck will suddenly free ourselves and finally
rake the life together, submitting to eternal chaos.

We'll sweep our lives like a pile of
bones, and make an even spine, and ribs,
and a skull, and all the tibia and radius bones,

without missing anything, and will finally find out
what kind of creature we are, what all of this is for
and where we all go, moving forward in space and
 time.

And we'll become strong, crispy, fresh,
like green apples; we will be arrogant, happy
and cheerful, and sometimes will call our mentors
to tell them that we miss them, like we miss dear
 home.
Will grow hair of the desired length in two hours in a
 special
chamber, and finally feel what fabulous luck it is to be
 so alive.

Messenger
~ n a spencer

To glimpse your shoulder
                        ever turning
Dayward toward the breaking light
At the terminus where dreaming
Falls off in echoes
              bending
The magnetic limbus of a frangible shore

Is to find myself surrendered
                        utterly
To your Otherness inside my marrow
A fragrance closer than thought
Like the skin
          of an empty
          luminous sky
Sundered of every innocence

Not the dream
              but breath of you
Forming the trajectory of my desire

Cloaked in smoke
              and wings
              of hummingbirds
Hovering about my head
And burning
            the sun inside my belly
Ripening to a corporeal dawn

Our Compound
John Philip Johnson

Franklin caught his brother
cutting the protective barbed-wire,
trying to get out. We were all
surprised by that and by
how Franklin raged at him,
given this was all supposed to be
about brotherly love. Then Franklin
locked him in the Bunker of Wellness,
even though he wasn't sick. We all
knew it was horrible in there.

We all wrote essays for days
trying to persuade Franklin
his brother was still one of us.
We came here for freedom, after all,
and moreover, our compound was
devoted 1. to the protection and well-
being of its members, 2. to the acquisition
of mystical truths, and 3. to the development
of our higher natures as we envisioned them.

Franklin would have none of it.
In fact, just when he seemed like
he'd had his fill of our delicate,
nuanced reasoning and was about
to respond, one of us, a woman,
we don't remember her name—
she had short, dark, curly hair—
started roaring like a lion
and laughing at the same time.

For a moment, Franklin was taken aback. We all stared at her. She was completely separate from us now, laughing at all of us. She seemed—well, palpable, in a funny way that was dangerous to everyone. The rest of us were still living the dream. She kept laughing, too, as he had her dragged to the bunker.

Abra-Cadaver
By Aurelio Rico Lopez III

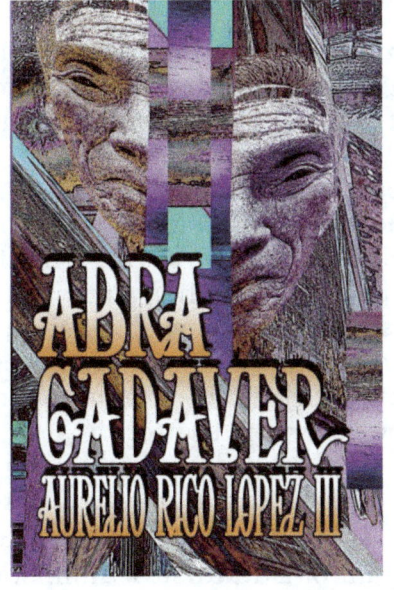

https://www.hiraethsffh.com/product-page/abra-cadaver-by-aurelio-rico-lopez-iii

Who?

Simon Kewin is the author of over 100 published short and flash stories. His works have appeared in Analog, Nature, Daily Science Fiction and many more. He is also the author of the Cloven Land fantasy trilogy, cyberpunk thriller The Genehunter, steampunk Gormenghast saga Engn, the Triple Stars sci/fi trilogy and the Office of the Witchfinder General books, published by Elsewhen Press. In 2022, he was an SPSFC semi-finalist and had a short story shortlisted for a Utopia award. He lives deep in the English countryside. Find him at simonkewin.co.uk and at @SimonKewin on Twitter.

n a spencer is a writer and artist based in Denver, Colorado. She's described her poetry as reflecting "a lived-in amalgam of Buddhist & animistic perspectives working itself out – less about me expressing myself than just coming to terms with my own astonishment at life."

Lisa Timpf is a retired HR and communications professional who lives in Simcoe, Ontario. When not writing, Lisa enjoys organic gardening, bird watching, and taking long walks with her cocker spaniel-Jack Russell mix Chet. Lisa's speculative fiction has appeared in *NewMyths,Home for the Howlidays, Cosmic Crime*, and other venues. Lisa's collection of speculative haibun poetry, *In Days to Come*, is available from Hiraeth Publishing. You can find out more about Lisa's writing at http://lisatimpf.blogspot.com/.

Frank Coffman is a retired professor of English, Creative Writing, and Journalism. He is a formalist poet, specializing in speculative poetry across the several genres of the high imagination—chiefly the Weird, Supernatural, Horrific, and Science Fictional. Although considering himself to be 'primarily a sonneteer,' his four collections of verse show his love of experimentation with form and the use of many exotic, cross-cultural, and invented 'shapes of singing,' including work in classical, medieval, renaissance, and modern forms.

John Philip Johnson has had science fiction and fantasy work in numerous venues and won a Pushcart Prize in 2021 for a genre poem. He has two comic books of graphic poetry, *Stairs Appear in a Hole Outside of Town* and *The Book of Fly*, the latter which won an Elgin Award. He would live on Mars if he could. johnphilipjohnson.com

www.ingramcontent.com/pod-product-compliance
Lightning Source LLC
LaVergne TN
LVHW020420070526
838199LV00055B/3673